TRINITY REPERTOIRE LIBRARY

the electronic keyboard collection book 2

Selected and edited by Jeremy Ward

Faber Music 3 Queen Square London WC1N 3AU
in association with
Trinity Guildhall 89 Albert Embankment London SE1 7TP

Contents

Can Can Offenbach *page 3*

Memory Lloyd Webber *page 4*

In the Shadows Ward *page 5*

Walking in the Air Blake *page 6*

Indian Summer Composition project *page 7*

You and You J Strauss II *page 8*

Jive at Five Ward *page 9*

Latin Lady Wedgwood *page 10*

Super Trouper Andersson/Ulvaeus *page 11*

Movie Magic Ward *page 12*

Take the Ghan Milne *page 13*

Parisienne Dreams Ward *page 14*

Theme of Peace Composition project *page 16*

© 2005 by Faber Music Ltd and Trinity College London
First published in 2005 by Faber Music Ltd
in association with Trinity College London
3 Queen Square London WC1N 3AU
Cover design by Sue Clarke
Music processed by Jackie Leigh
Printed in England by Caligraving Ltd
All rights reserved

ISBN10: 0-571-52353-6
EAN13: 978-0-571-52353-5

To buy Faber Music or Trinity publications or to find out about the full range of titles
available please contact your local music retailer or Faber Music sales enquiries:

Faber Music Ltd, Burnt Mill, Elizabeth Way, Harlow CM20 2HX
Tel: +44 (0)1279 82 89 82   Fax: +44 (0)1279 82 89 83
sales@fabermusic.com   www.fabermusic.com   www.trinityguildhall.co.uk

Can Can

Jacques Offenbach (arr. Ward)

Voice: Vibraphone/Clarinet
Style: Polka

This famous dance suits the glockenspiel (vibraphone) voice; make sure the notes are crisp and even. Adding the clarinet on the octave doubling helps to give the line emphasis. Try adding different accompaniments and also changing octaves to give extra colour and interest.

© 2005 by Faber Music Ltd and Trinity College London

Memory

Music by Andrew Lloyd Webber (arr. Ward)
Text by Trevor Nunn after T. S. Eliot

Voice: Oboe/Strings
Style: Ballad

This is the most popular tune from Andrew Lloyd Webber's musical 'Cats'. The melody should be smooth and well-phrased, as it would be sung. The middle section should sound fuller, with a little more movement. Try adding another accompaniment level when the tune returns in the new key.

In the Shadows

Jeremy Ward

Voice: Clean Guitar
Style: 60s Pop

This is inspired by the 1960s band The Shadows. Imagine you are at the front of the band playing to a large audience. The eighth notes (quavers) need to bounce along, and the rests are important, adding rhythmic interest.

Walking in the Air

'The Snowman'

Howard Blake (arr. Ward)

Voice: Oboe/Piano, Strings
Style: Ballad

This is theme from the film 'The Snowman'. The lyrics to the song are about flying, so the melody must flow as if you are floating. Look out for opportunities to add extra ideas in accompaniment and voices. Try to find a voice on your keyboard that captures the spirit of a cold winter's night.

© 1982 by Highbridge Music Ltd. All Rights Reserved

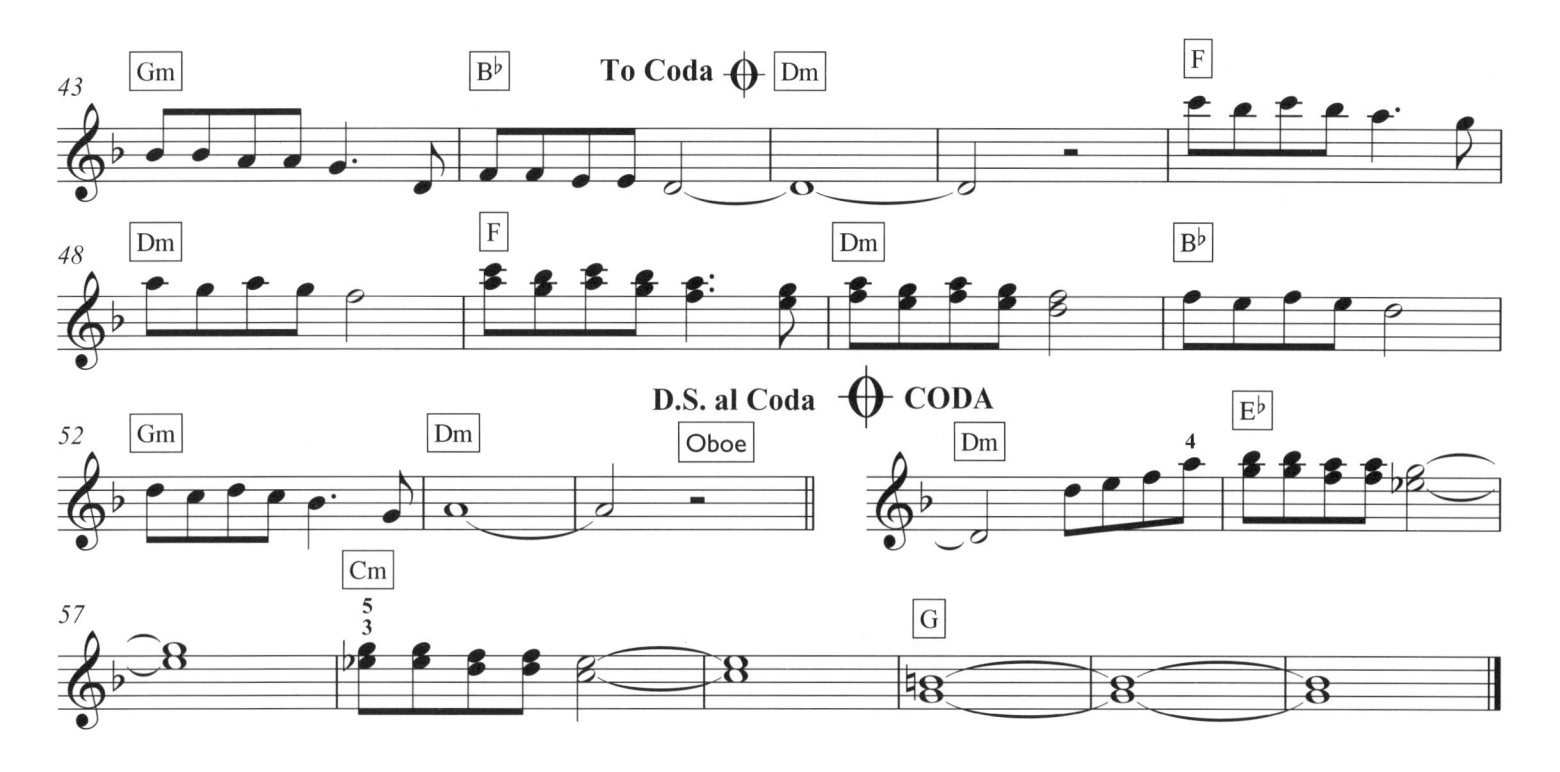

Indian Summer

Composition project

Voice: Own Choice
Style: Own Choice

You need to select a voice, style and dynamics and also develop some ideas to make this piece complete. The music is based on an Indian scale called a *raga* (the notes are given below): try to use only these notes for your new ideas. Keep the Indian flavour in the choice of voice, but also add other voices to give contrast. Try putting phrases up an octave as well.

Tranquilly ♩ = 120-140

Add your own ideas

Add your own ideas

Add your own ideas

You and You

Johann Strauss II (arr. Ward)

Voice: Flute/Strings
Style: Viennese Waltz

Strauss was known as the King of Waltz; everyone wanted to hear his music and dance to his tunes. This waltz needs excitement and movement; the flute adds a light and agile feel to the melody, but don't forget to phrase it so the player can breathe! When the strings come in, try to *crescendo* and build to the climax.

Jive at Five

Jeremy Ward

Voice: Tenor Sax/Brass Combo
Style: Big Band

Jive was a dance craze in the 1950s; it meant a lot of jumping and twisting, which is why this is in swing time. You must take care of the rests as this is where the jumping takes place.

Latin Lady

Pam Wedgwood

Voice: Trumpet
Style: Slow Samba

This Latin dance is portrayed by the moody trumpet voice. This piece needs to be played rhythmically with a good feeling of phrasing.

Super Trouper

Benny Andersson/Bjoern Ulvaeus (arr. Ward)

Voice: Big Lead/Strings
Style: Hard Rock

This needs to have a driving feel, but don't rush the opening. The middle section, played on strings, needs to have the feel of *legato* bowing. You can add a lot of extra accompaniment levels to make a difference between sections, but save the big one for the D.S.

© Copyright Bocu Music Ltd, 1 Wyndham Yard, London W1H 2QF by permission.
This arrangement © 2005 Bocu Music Ltd

Movie Magic

Jeremy Ward

Voice: Atmosphere or any synth voice/Strings
Style: Secret Service Ballad or Rock

This is a theme tune to a blockbuster spy movie! Create the suspense through the short repeated idea at the start. The middle section is a chase and the *staccatos* are the bullets! The melody is the love interest reflected by the smooth string sound.

Take the Ghan

Elissa Milne

Voice: Piano/Brass
Style: Swing

This is a rip roaring trip on an Australian train through the fantastic scenery. The opening is the train already at full speed; the rests give the feeling of speed and scenery flashing by. The eighth notes (quavers) in bar 9 are the train's whistle – letting people and kangaroos know the train is coming!

Parisienne Dreams

Jeremy Ward

Voice: Accordion/Strings
Style: Guitar Serenade or Light Waltz

This piece was inspired by a walk along the River Seine in Paris. Paris is a very romantic city and the accordion voice is intended to capture that and the Gallic feel. It should be played very smoothly; try adding small accompaniment variations to create swells.

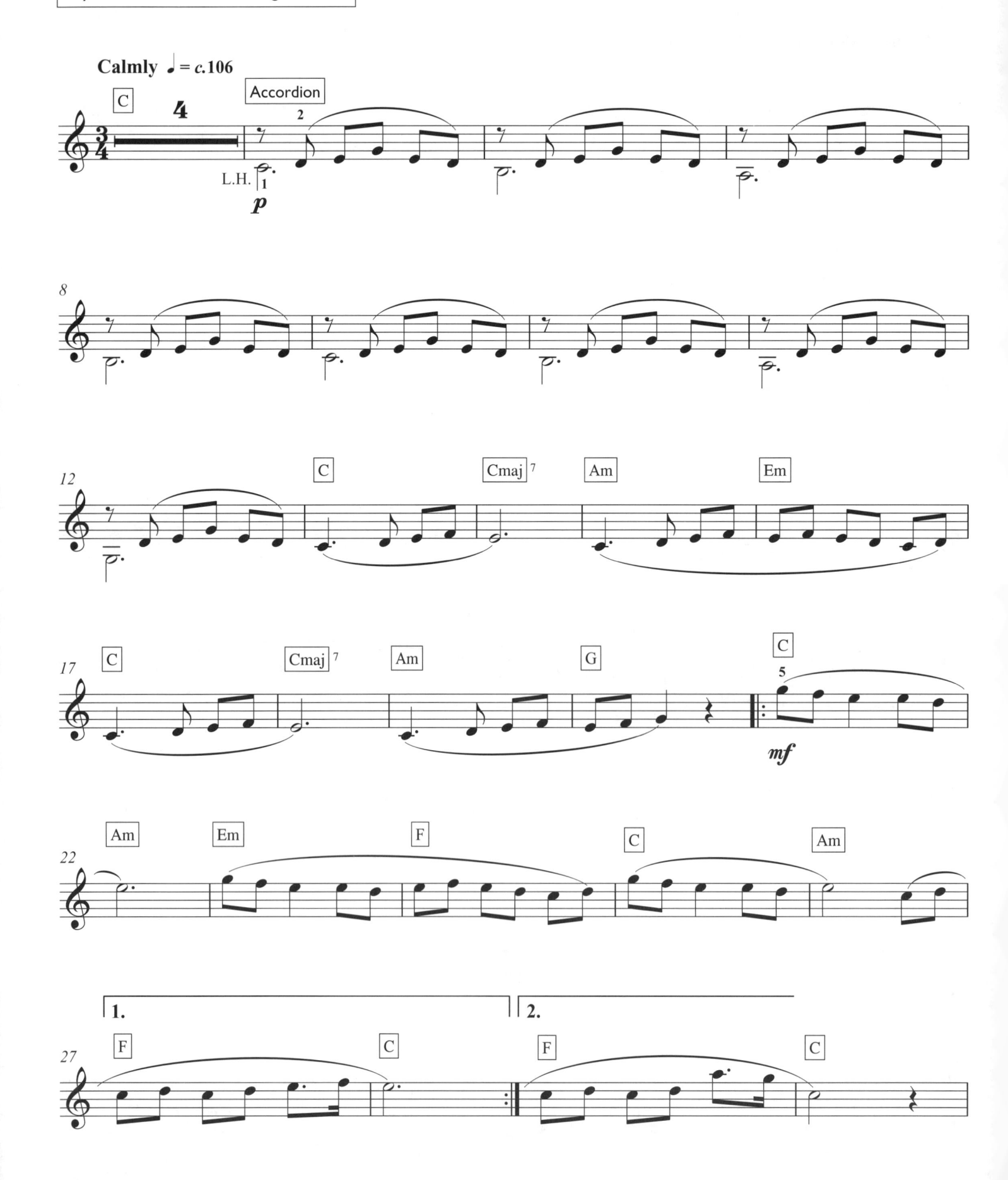

Add Strings
Dm
G
C
F
G
C
Cmaj 7
Dm
G
C
F
G
C
Am
Em
F
C
Am
F
C
Strings off
L.H.
C
Dm
F
C

Theme of Peace

Composition project

Voice: Own Choice
Style: Own Choice

In this piece you need to compose some additional material and select your own style, voice and dynamics. Remember to keep to the given idea and see if the chord sequence is similar to anything that has gone before. Choose the style and voice to reflect the title: perhaps a string sound and ballad style.

Peacefully ♩ = 80-100

Add your own ideas

Add your own ideas